797,885 Books
are available to read at

Forgotten Books

www.ForgottenBooks.com

Forgotten Books' App
Available for mobile, tablet & eReader

ISBN 978-0-243-32865-9
PIBN 10793793

This book is a reproduction of an important historical work. Forgotten Books uses state-of-the-art technology to digitally reconstruct the work, preserving the original format whilst repairing imperfections present in the aged copy. In rare cases, an imperfection in the original, such as a blemish or missing page, may be replicated in our edition. We do, however, repair the vast majority of imperfections successfully; any imperfections that remain are intentionally left to preserve the state of such historical works.

Forgotten Books is a registered trademark of FB &c Ltd.
Copyright © 2017 FB &c Ltd.
FB &c Ltd, Dalton House, 60 Windsor Avenue, London, SW19 2RR.
Company number 08720141. Registered in England and Wales.

For support please visit www.forgottenbooks.com

1 MONTH OF FREE READING

at

www.ForgottenBooks.com

By purchasing this book you are eligible for one month membership to ForgottenBooks.com, giving you unlimited access to our entire collection of over 700,000 titles via our web site and mobile apps.

To claim your free month visit:
www.forgottenbooks.com/free793793

* Offer is valid for 45 days from date of purchase. Terms and conditions apply.

English
Français
Deutsche
Italiano
Español
Português

www.forgottenbooks.com

Mythology Photography **Fiction**
Fishing Christianity **Art** Cooking
Essays Buddhism Freemasonry
Medicine **Biology** Music **Ancient Egypt** Evolution Carpentry Physics
Dance Geology **Mathematics** Fitness
Shakespeare **Folklore** Yoga Marketing
Confidence Immortality Biographies
Poetry **Psychology** Witchcraft
Electronics Chemistry History **Law**
Accounting **Philosophy** Anthropology
Alchemy Drama Quantum Mechanics
Atheism Sexual Health **Ancient History**
Entrepreneurship Languages Sport
Paleontology Needlework Islam
Metaphysics Investment Archaeology
Parenting Statistics Criminology
Motivational

C 7342.527

Harvard College Library

BOUGHT FROM THE
**ANDREW PRESTON PEABODY
FUND**

BEQUEATHED BY
CAROLINE EUSTIS PEABODY
OF CAMBRIDGE

CONCERNING

WILLIAM BYRD;

AND ONE CONCERNING

ANN BREWSTER.

PRINTED BY DIRECTION OF THE YEARLY MEETING
OF FRIENDS, HELD IN LONDON,
1836.

LONDON:
PRINTED FOR DARTON AND HARVEY,
GRACECHURCH STREET.
—
MDCCCXXXVI.

C 8342.528

Harvard University Library
Feb 3, 1942

Peabody fd.

A TESTIMONY

From the MONTHLY MEETING *of* SHAFTESBURY *and* SHERBORNE, *in the* COUNTY OF DORSET, *respecting* WILLIAM BYRD, *of* MARNHULL, *deceased.*

OUR ancient friend, WILLIAM BYRD, departed this life at Marnhull, on the 16th of the twelfth month, 1835, in the seventy-eighth year of his age, and was interred in Friends' burying-ground at Marnhull, on the 22d of the same, having been a Minister about forty-three years.

In bearing our testimony to the Christian character and religious services of our dear friend, we trust we may be allowed to apply to him the words of Holy Scripture, respecting a servant of the Lord, in days of old, that he was " a faithful man, and feared God above many." We counted him an Elder worthy of double honour : and he was beloved amongst us as a father in Christ.

Of his early life we have not been able to

gather many particulars. He was born at Uffculm, in the county of Devon, in the year 1757; his parents, who were members of our religious society, were concerned for his education consistently with our Christian profession. In his youth, though it is believed that he was much preserved from the corruptions of the world, yet he occasionally deviated from the plainness in which he had been brought up; but being favoured with serious religious impressions, he soon adopted the simple habits of Friends. In recurring, in after life, to these early acts of obedience, he thought he could perceive cause to believe that they were owned by tokens of Divine approbation. About the twenty-second year of his age he left home, and became an assistant in business to a friend at Long-ham, in the county of Dorset: whilst living in that situation he is remembered as a young man of decidedly religious character, and of circumspect conduct; and there is strong reason to believe that the work of the Lord was, at that time, making progress in his heart. In the course of about two years, he removed to the village of Marnhull, and entered into business, upon a small scale, as a shopkeeper: it is the testimony of those who were then acquainted with him, and who had the opportunity of marking his subsequent walk in life, that in conducting his concerns in trade, in his deportment in private life, and in his intercourse with the world, it appeared to be his earnest and unremitting exercise, to have a conscience void of offence toward God and toward men. He was scrupulously upright in all his transactions; and, though far from indifferent to the importance of obtaining a comfortable iudependence in life, as well as to the means of contributing to the relief of the wants of others, it was evident that his affections were set upon things above rather than on things on the earth; this was remarkably exemplified not only by his constant attendance of meetings for Divine worship, but by his concern that the different members of his family might enjoy the same privilege: with this view he thought it right, even, when in very limited circumstances, to shut up his shop during the time of the week-day meeting. This, he remarks, in a memorandum made about that time, was when he did not know it to be the practice of any other friend in the nation. After having been a few years in trade, in grateful record of the goodness of Divine Providence, he notices the blessing which had rested upon his honest endeavours: "Very little," says he, "had I to begin with in business something "less than four years since, in which time I "have gained, I believe, at least five times the "sum with which I began."

The Holy Scriptures were precious to him, and he was at that time punctual in collecting his family every evening for the reading of them; and it was observed that he regularly set apart a portion of the day for private religious retirement, a practice in which he continued to old age. As he grew in grace, and became increasingly subjected to the government of the Holy Spirit, he was gradually prepared for usefulness in the Church; and in the thirty-fifth year of his age he came forwards as a Minister amongst us. He appears to have entered upon the service in fear and much trembling; and he was frequent in awful and reverent waiting upon God, in a watchful and teachable spirit, that he might be instructed to the knowledge of his will in this great duty, and be preserved under the safe leading of the Heavenly Shepherd. He was sound in doctrine, and his ministry was exercised in simplicity, and in demonstration of the Spirit and of power. He sought not the praise of men; but in the exercise of the gift that had been bestowed upon him, he humbly and honestly endeavoured to approve himself faithful to his great Lord and Master in the work to which he had been pleased to appoint him.

In the year 1800, he was married to our friend Rebecca Young, of Shrewsbury. In her, he found a companion well prepared to unite with him in a self-denying course of Christian dedication: and, we believe, it is not too much to say, respecting our beloved friends, that it was their daily concern, like Zecharias and Elizabeth, to walk together in all the commandments and ordinances of the Lord blameless; and having, each of them, received a dispensation of the gospel, they sought to adorn the doctrine of God our Saviour in all things. They were examples amongst us of a cheerful contentment, in the plainness of the furniture of their house, in the simplicity of their mode of life, and in the moderation of their expenses. Their means were at no time abundant, but they were kind and liberal to the poor, generous in their hospitality, and especially engaged to help and succour those who came amongst us in the work of the ministry. They had, both of them, been brought into much religious concern on account of the continuance of the African Slave Trade, and the subsequent slavery of its victims. From early life they had individually thought it laid upon them, as a testimony against that unrighteous gain of oppression, to abstain from the use of the produce of West India Slavery; and our friend, William Byrd, almost from the first of his going into business, and at a considerable loss of profit, refused to deal in articles of that description. They took a deep interest in those measures which, under the blessing of the Lord, tended to the abolition of the Slave Trade; and after many years of sorrow and suffering, in sympathy with this afflicted portion of our fellow-creatures, they lived to rejoice in the Act of our Legislature, by which Slavery was declared to be illegal throughout the British dominions; and though, at that time, far advanced in age and much worn by sickness and infirmity, their sympathies were still alive to the degradation and oppressive servitude which a large proportion of the Negroes continued to suffer in our Colonial possessions.

For several years the Ministry of our dear friend was much confined within the limits of this county and parts adjacent. On his marriage he was not only concerned to encourage his wife in her devotedness to the cause of our Holy Redeemer; but frequently accompanied her in her travels, and for many years they were extensively engaged in the work of the Gospel, in various parts of this nation, and in Ireland, and he bore her company in her second visit to the Orkney Islands. They laboured diligently both among friends and the people at large, and we have reason to believe that his service on these occasions, and his humble, simple, watchful deportment were acceptable and instructive. He highly valued the various Christian testimonies of our religious society, and was zealously concerned that they might be faithfully and uprightly supported by friends everywhere. He was frequently at the Yearly Meeting, and thought it a privilege to be allowed to unite with his brethren for the increase of vital Christianity amongst us;

and, though a man of good understanding, and deep experience, he was not forward in giving his judgment; but when he offered an opinion, it was with weight and to the purpose. He was a lover of good men of every denomination, and of enlarged charity, and liberal views; tender towards such as had been overtaken in a fault; never seeming to forget that he himself was liable to temptation; and patient in labour for the restoration of transgressors. In the general exercise of the discipline in our Monthly Meetings, of which he was constant in his attendance for nearly fifty years, he was religiously concerned that it might be administered in the meekness of wisdom, without partiality, and to the honour of the cause of Truth: that this was the exercise of his mind to the close of life, is apparent by the following remarks which he dictated after he became confined to his bed.

26th Twelfth Month, 1833.—'Sometime after awaking this morning, I had sweetly to recollect some expressions of Jonah Thompson, when near the close of life, which I thought might, in measure, be applicable to myself; that he had in possession, "a quiet, easy mind, and no accuser "there;" but, alas, different thoughts occurred: I remembered, that in transacting the discipline of the Church, I had but too often engaged therein without waiting for a proper qualification. Under these different cogitations, I recollected the following expressions of John Griffiths: " The true "labourer must in every meeting, and upon all "occasions that offer for service, receive super-"natural aid, and a renewed understanding by " the immediate descending of Heavenly power " and wisdom, or he dare not meddle :" although I am not without hope, (that) I shall be forgiven in the day of account for this, and other deviations, yet I am persuaded, had I thus steered my course, my engagements in that line would have been attended with more peace to my mind, and been more to the promotion of the cause of Truth.'

As he advanced in life, our beloved friend did not lose sight of his own infirmity, and we believe that, through the help of the Lord, he did not cease to press towards the mark that had been set before him. Christ was precious to his soul, and he gave satisfactory evidence, even in old age, that in a broken and contrite spirit he rested on his Saviour alone for the forgiveness of his sins, and his final acceptance. The following extracts from his papers, as they are descriptive of his religious exercise, are, we think, worthy of preservation.

11th First Month, 1811.—' What watchfulness and prayer are necessary, in order to our meeting every event, whether prosperous or adverse, with that humility and dependence, that patience, meekness, and calm resignation which become the professed followers, and more especially the Ministers of the Captain of our Salvation, (of Him) who took upon himself the form of a servant,—made himself of no reputation—was meek and lowly in heart—" endured the cross and de-" spised the shame; and left us an example that " we should follow his steps."

24th Tenth Month, 1820.—' In our week-day Meeting, the query revived in my mind, " What lack I yet?" and the answer of my heart seemed to be; more reverent watchfulness, more meekness, more patience, more faith, and more of that charity "which beareth all things, believeth all things, hopeth all things, endureth all things, and never faileth."

30th Fourth Month, 1824.—'Oh! saith my soul, may the watch be so maintained in reverential fear, (and in the) meekness and patience of Jesus, that preparation and a growth in the Truth may be my continued experience, to the end of my days.'

For the last four years of his life, the health of our dear friend was much impaired, and it repeatedly appeared to those around him, that his end was fast approaching. During this long confinement his mental powers occasionally failed him, but his recollection was often clear; and he was able to take enjoyment in the society of his friends and near connexions. He was kept in a lowly, watchful, and dependent mind, often numbering his blessings, and with much tenderness of spirit acknowledging to the kindness and love of our Heavenly Father. He had been accustomed to look upon himself but as a steward over the bounty of a gracious Providence towards him; and when after his own wants, which were few, had been supplied, he could not rest satisfied till the surplus was distributed among his poor neighbours. On one of these occasions, not long before his death, on its being observed that he might need it for himself, he replied with earnestness, " We must spend it, or it will be a burthen " greater than I can bear."

Lon after he was unable to read he derived much comfort from having the Holy Scriptures read to him; and in those times which were devoted to retirement before the Lord, and they were frequent, it was observed by his niece that he often appeared to be engaged in prayer and thanksgiving. On one occasion, in the early part of his illness, he told those who were attending upon him, that he had been much comforted, and thought he had never been nearer the Lord. One of his relations some time afterwards going into the room and enquiring how he was, he answered, " Pretty much " the same;—feeble.—I have had a tendering sea- " son, and thought all my sins were forgiven me." The next morning he seemed to be much favoured with a sense of the presence of his Saviour, and said he thought he was (drawing) nearer his desired haven, that he was in peace with all men, and had nothing to do but to die. After having been in a very low state of mind for several days, on being asked how he was, he said, " More comfortable;" and added that he did not expect such comfort before he went hence : and in much brokenness of spirit, he added; " Oh, " what shall I render to the Lord for all his mer- " cies ?" On another occasion in grateful retrospect of the goodness of God towards him, he observed; "Great have been the mercies of my "Heavenly Father from my youth up: had he "not placed his fear in my heart, I had long since "been a cast-away." On being informed that it was First Day, he said, "O that it may be "well spent." A little afterwards, "I cannot "keep up the exercise I could wish; I have great "weakness both in body and mind." On being helped up in bed, he remarked, "A posture for "dying: see with what peace a Christian can "die—there is nothing in my way:" and having spoken in testimony to the truth as it is in Jesus, he concluded with the language of praise, "Bless "the Lord, O my soul; and all that is within me "bless his Holy Name." Such expressions as the following, uttered at different times, indicate that his mind was still stayed on God:—"Oh, the "sweet peaceful feeling I have this evening, I "would not exchange it for all the kingdoms of "this world." At another time: "A calm and "peaceful mind: how precious!" and again: "Lord, now let thy servant depart in peace, for "mine eyes have seen thy salvation." Thus it was evident, to use his own words, that "death had no terrors for him." He continued in the same tender, submissive, hopeful, and child-like state to the end; and at length suddenly and unexpectedly passed away, with very little apparent suffering.

Our dear departed friend having loved and honoured his Lord and Saviour upon earth, and it having been his chief concern in life to watch and to keep his garments, we reverently trust that, through the riches of redeeming grace, it has been given him to join the spirits of just men made perfect in the presence of God and of the Lamb.

Read, approved, and signed in our Monthly Meeting, held at Shaftesbury, the 5th of 4th mo. 1836. *(Here follow the signatures of men and women friends.)*

At a General Meeting for Dorset and Hants, held at Poole, the 7th of 4th month, 1836,

The foregoing Testimony respecting our dear deceased friend, William Byrd, has been read, with which this Meeting fully unites, and desires that the example of our dear friend in his Christian life and conversation, and in his peaceful end, may continue to live in our remembrance.

Signed in and on behalf of the General Meeting,

SAMUEL HANNAM, *Clerk.*

A TESTIMONY

Of KINGSTON MONTHLY MEETING, *in the* COUNTY OF SURREY, *concerning* ANN BREWSTER *of* CLAPHAM, *deceased*.

In the remembrance of the humility and dedication to the cause of truth and righteousness which characterized this our beloved friend, evidenced by yielding obedience to the restraining and tendering operations of Divine grace, we feel engaged to give forth a testimony concerning her, in the hope that her example may have an animating influence on survivors, holding forth this language, Follow me as I have endeavoured to follow Christ.

She was the daughter of Edward and Sarah Shewell, and was born in London in the year 1762. The religious care exercised by her parents over the minds of their tender offspring appears, as she expresses it, to have been "so far blessed to some of them that it proved as a nail fastened in a sure place." We cannot more appropriately set forth the experience of our dear friend, than by some extracts from her own memoranda. In these she remarks, "I could say with thankfulness of heart the Lord was my morning Light; for I well remember to have been favoured with that light in very early life as a reprover for sin, even in childish transgressions and disobedience to parental injunctions. Thus it was with me," she adds, "when very young, that I was made renewedly sensible of the love of Him who first loved us; and I often shed tears of joy under a sense of the power of Divine love covering my mind in a remarkable manner, so that I loved to get alone to enjoy the inexpressible comfort I derived from it, and this brought a great fear and dread over my mind, lest I should offend Him whom I loved and fervently desired would not overlook such a poor little child. When I committed a fault, how keenly have I felt reproof. I am certain that if the necessity of attending to the inward monitor were impressed upon children, they would not so often grow up in hardness of heart."

When about seven years of age she was sent to a boarding-school, where, in endeavouring to maintain her consistency as a Friend, by using the plain language, (being the only Friend's child there,) she became subject to ridicule from some of her companions; but, she remarks, "there were other dear children to whom I was affectionately attached and united, whose minds were remarkably visited by the influences of the Holy Spirit, by which we were drawn to read the Holy Scriptures together, and converse upon them with great interest."

Although love to her Heavenly Father thus prevailed in her heart, yet as she grew older, through drawing back from His restraining power, she wished for more liberty in dress and some other things; but, she observes, "loving-kindness followed me, so that I found a place of prayer in secret; and I can now say that I loved the Lord my God, and Jesus Christ his beloved Son, my Redeemer; for I have been sensible of the inshinings of heavenly love at times, throughout my life." In another place she says, "I remember one of my schoolfellows describing some places of amusement, which raised something like a regret that I could not go, when the words arose in my mind, 'They that love anything more than me, are not worthy of me,' filling me with sweet peace, so that I never afterwards felt even a desire after anything of this kind : and now I can say I am thankful for having been brought up amongst Friends, a people whose principles are pure, and though they bring into the narrow way, yet is that way quite broad enough to walk in and enjoy the blessings of life."

Our dear friend was united in marriage with Thomas Brewster in the year 1784, and came to reside within the limits of this Monthly Meeting in 1800. Her disposition was remarkably tender and humane, and evinced much sympathy with those under suffering. She was ever ready to relieve the wants of the poor, and she discharged the various relative duties of life with much affectionate kindness.

From 1812 to 1828, she continued at times to record in her diary her various trials and religious exercises, particularly relating to her being called to the work of the ministry, which laid weightily on her mind for many years. At length, believing the time to be arrived, the natural timidity of her disposition gave way to apprehended duty, and she expressed a few words in the Meeting at Wandsworth in the 12th month, 1818, and it appears to have afforded her sweet peace in thus submitting her will to that of her Divine Master. On this occasion she writes, "I hope I shall be strengthened to praise His holy name on a dying bed for all his mercies towards me, an unworthy creature."

In 1821, she was acknowledged as a minister, and in the same year paid a religious visit to the families of Friends of Wandsworth particular Meeting; in yielding to which service, heavenly peace appears to have been her portion. She was subsequently engaged in several visits to her own and some of the neighbouring Quarterly Meetings, from which labours of love she also experienced much comfort, saying, on one occasion, "I have great cause to commemorate the Lord's favours." In the course of a visit she paid in 1825 to the families of Friends in one of the Monthly Meetings in Suffolk, she mentions, "She had times of discouragement and suffering, from a sense of great weakness, crying, 'Lord increase my faith, and arise for my help; preserve me that so thy precious cause may never suffer through me a poor worm.'" Her communications in the exercise of her gift, though short, were lively and marked by much simplicity and sweetness; the love of our Heavenly Father appeared to be the constant clothing of her mind.

In the 4th month, 1828, she was attacked with chronic rheumatism, which produced great suffering for the remainder of her life, during which much patience and resignation were manifest.

She was a diligent attender of our religious Meetings, and in them was often favoured with a renewal of her strength; she continued in the performance of this duty even when her bodily infirmities rendered her unable to move without assistance; and when wholly prevented from thus meeting with her friends, she considered this to be the greatest privation it was her lot to experience. During this latter period the Monthly Meetings for Ministers and Elders were chiefly held in her chamber, a privilege she highly valued; the remembrance thereof by those who met on these occasions is sweet, so remarkably did they appear to be times of the overshadowing of Divine love.

The bodily sufferings of this our dear friend during the last year of her life were very great;

but she was enabled to bear them with Christian patience, and in humble resignation to wait the Lord's time, whilst the earnest desire of her heart was to be permitted at last to reach a place of rest and peace, " where," she adds, " I shall meet my dear Lord, and live for ever with him! then shall I attain unto the consummate wishes and breathings of my soul through life, having had an earnest desire to be found worthy to be admitted an inhabitant in the kingdom of Heaven, when time shall terminate my existence here."

Thus our beloved friend was preserved in faith and patience to the end: and when He whose tender love had followed her all her life, and through whose strength she had been enabled to occupy the talent received, was pleased to say, It is enough! and to remove her from this state of probation and suffering, we reverently believe the ardent prayer of her soul was answered, and that, through redeeming love and mercy, she is admitted into the joy of her Lord.

Our dear friend died on the 21st of 4th month, 1835, and her remains were interred at Croydon, on the 29th of the same; aged seventy-three years. A Minister about sixteen years.

Signed in Kingston Monthly Meeting, held at Wandsworth, the 19th of the 11th month, 1835. *(Here follow the signatures of men and women Friends.)*

Read and approved in our Quarterly Meeting for London and Middlesex, held this 29th day of the 12th month, 1835; and in and on behalf thereof signed, by

GEORGE STACEY, *Clerk.*

Signed in and on behalf of the Women's Meeting, by

RACHEL STACEY, *Clerk.*

CPSIA information can be obtained
at www.ICGtesting.com
Printed in the USA
BVHW060923140119
537775BV00010B/1915/P